FOREST FOOD CHAINS

Bobbie Kalman

Crabtree Publishing Company

www.crabtreebooks.com

Created by Bobbie Kalman

Dedicated by Kristina Lundblad
For my sister and best friend, Katarina. You're a food chain.

Author and Editor-in-Chief
Bobbie Kalman

Substantive editor
Kathryn Smithyman

Project editor and research
Kristina Lundblad

Editors
Molly Aloian
Kelley MacAulay

Art director
Robert MacGregor

Design
Katherine Kantor

Production coordinator
Katherine Kantor

Photo research
Crystal Foxton

Consultant
Patricia Loesche, Ph.D., Animal Behavior Program,
Department of Psychology, University of Washington

Photographs
All images by Adobe Image Library, Corbis, Corel, Creatas,
Digital Stock, and Digital Vision

Illustrations
Barbara Bedell: pages 3 (mink, cardinal, leaves, hedgehog,
    squirrel, and woodpecker), 4 (leaves), 7 (plant-left, mouse, and
    coyote), 8-9 (all except eagle, deer, tree-far left and middle, fern,
    and plants-page 9 bottom left and right), 12, 13, 16, 20 (weasel),
    21, 22, 24 (all except earthworm), 26 (all except nuts and wolf), 27
Katherine Kantor: pages 8-9 (deer), 15, 18, 26 (nuts)
Ellen O'Hara: page 4 (cone and needles)
Margaret Amy Reiach: series logo, pages 7 (sun), 8-9 (tree-middle),
    10, 24 (earthworm), 26 (wolf), 29
Bonna Rouse: pages 3 (mushrooms, fern, beaver, and tree),
    4 (moss, fern, and trees), 7 (plant-right), 8-9 (eagle, tree-far left,
    fern, and plants-page 9 bottom left and right), 17, 20 (eagles), 31

Crabtree Publishing Company

www.crabtreebooks.com   1-800-387-7650

Copyright © **2005 CRABTREE PUBLISHING COMPANY**.
All rights reserved. No part of this publication may be
reproduced, stored in a retrieval system or be transmitted in
any form or by any means, electronic, mechanical, photocopying,
recording, or otherwise, without the prior written permission
of Crabtree Publishing Company. In Canada: We acknowledge the
financial support of the Government of Canada through the Book
Publishing Industry Development Program (BPIDP) for our
publishing activities.

Cataloging-in-Publication Data
Kalman, Bobbie.
  Forest food chains / Bobbie Kalman.
    p. cm. -- (Food chains series)
  Includes index.
    ISBN 0-7787-1943-X (RLB) -- ISBN 0-7787-1989-8 (pbk.)
  1. Forest ecology--Juvenile literature. 2. Food chains
(Ecology)--Juvenile literature. I. Title.
  QH541.5.F6K344 2005
  577.3--dc22
                                                            2004013377
                                                                  LC

Published in
the United States
PMB16A
350 Fifth Ave.
Suite 3308
New York, NY
10118

Published
in Canada
616 Welland Ave.,
St. Catharines, Ontario
Canada
L2M 5V6

Published in the
United Kingdom
73 Lime Walk
Headington
Oxford
OX3 7AD
United Kingdom

Published
in Australia
386 Mt. Alexander Rd.,
Ascot Vale (Melbourne)
VIC 3032

Contents

What is a forest?

Ferns grow on the ground in forests.

Mosses grow on logs and rocks.

broadleaved tree *coniferous tree*

maple leaf

pine cone and leaves

A **forest** is a natural area where many trees grow. Forests are not just made up of trees, however. They include smaller plants, such as shrubs, **mosses**, and **ferns**. Some forests surround lakes, and some have rivers or streams running through them. Many kinds of animals live in forests.

Types of trees

There are two main types of trees— **broadleaved trees** or **broadleafs**, and **coniferous trees** or **conifers**. Broadleafs, such as maple trees, have flat, wide leaves with **veins**. Conifers, such as pine trees, have cones and needle-shaped leaves. Some forests have only conifers, whereas others have only broadleafs. **Mixed forests**, such as the one on page 5, have both types of trees.

4

Different kinds of forests

Forests in the northern parts of the world contain mainly conifers. They are called **boreal forests** or **taiga**. **Rain forests** grow in areas that are warm and rainy year-round. **Tropical rain forests** grow near the **equator** and have mostly broadleaved trees.

Temperate forests

Areas of the world that are cold for part of the year and warm for the rest of the year are known as **temperate** areas. The forests that grow in temperate areas are called **temperate forests**. Most temperate forests are mixed forests, but a few are made up mainly of conifers. This book is about food chains in temperate forests.

Mixed forests grow in parts of the world with four seasons: winter, spring, summer, and autumn.

What is a food chain?

This pileated woodpecker gets nutrients and energy by eating insects that live in the bark of trees.

Plants and animals are living things. All living things on Earth need air, water, sunlight, and food to survive. They get the **nutrients** they need from food. Nutrients are substances plants and animals need to grow and to stay healthy.

Energy for animals

Food also provides animals with **energy**. Animals use energy to breathe air, to grow, and to move from place to place.

Energy for plants

Plants do not eat to get energy from food. They **produce**, or make, their own food using the sun's energy!

Food chains

Animals must eat other living things to get energy. Some animals eat plants, whereas others eat animals that feed on plants. The pattern of eating and being eaten is called a **food chain**. An example of one food chain includes plants, a mouse, and a coyote—mice eat plants, and coyotes eat mice. All plants and animals belong to at least one food chain. Look at the diagram on the right to see how food chains work.

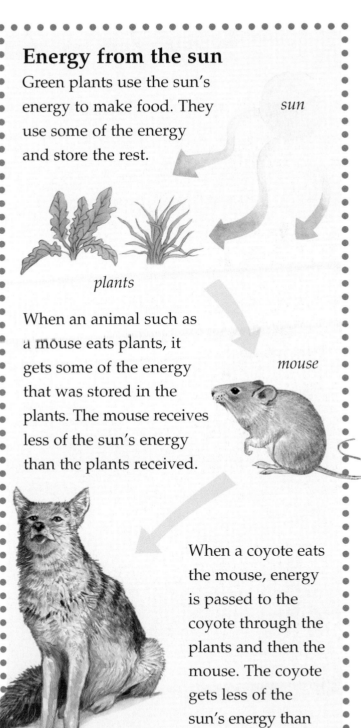

Energy from the sun

Green plants use the sun's energy to make food. They use some of the energy and store the rest.

sun

plants

When an animal such as a mouse eats plants, it gets some of the energy that was stored in the plants. The mouse receives less of the sun's energy than the plants received.

mouse

When a coyote eats the mouse, energy is passed to the coyote through the plants and then the mouse. The coyote gets less of the sun's energy than the mouse got.

coyote

An energy pyramid

As animals eat living things, their bodies take in energy. Energy is passed from one living thing to another. The energy flows in a pattern that is shown in the **energy pyramid** on the right. The first level of the pyramid is wide to show that there are many plants that make food energy. The second level is narrower because there are fewer animals than plants. The top level contains even fewer animals.

Third level: carnivores

The third level of a food chain is made up of **carnivores**. Carnivores are animals that get energy by eating other animals. Carnivores are the **secondary consumers** in a food chain.

Secondary consumers eat primary consumers. They are at the top of the food chain, where there is less of the sun's energy. For this reason, there are fewer carnivores than there are herbivores or plants.

Second level: herbivores

The second level of a food chain is made up of **herbivores**. Herbivores are animals that eat mainly plants. Herbivores are the **primary consumers** in a food chain.

Primary consumers are the first living things in a food chain that must eat to get energy. Herbivores must eat many plants to get the energy they need to survive. For this reason, there are fewer herbivores than there are plants.

First level: plants

The **primary**, or first, level of a food chain is made up of plants. Plants are called **primary producers** because they make food and are the first link in a food chain. There are more plants than there are animals. It takes many plants to feed all the animals in a food chain!

9

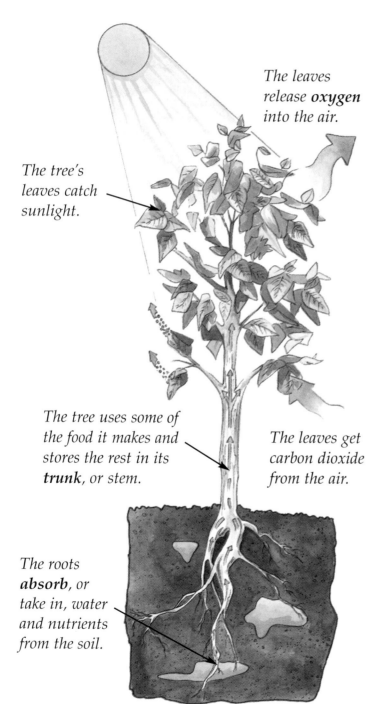

Food from the sun

*The leaves release **oxygen** into the air.*

The tree's leaves catch sunlight.

*The tree uses some of the food it makes and stores the rest in its **trunk**, or stem.*

The leaves get carbon dioxide from the air.

*The roots **absorb**, or take in, water and nutrients from the soil.*

Plants use the sun's energy to make food. They are the only living things that can make their own food. Making food from sunlight is called **photosynthesis**.

Making food

Plants have green **pigments**, or colors, called **chlorophyll** in their leaves. Chlorophyll catches sunlight to make food. It makes food by combining sunlight with water from the soil and **carbon dioxide**, a gas that is part of the air. A plant's food is called **glucose**, which is a type of sugar. Plants use some of the food they make and store the rest.

Plants help animals

Photosynthesis helps animals by using up some carbon dioxide from the air. Too much carbon dioxide can harm animals. Green plants also make large amounts of oxygen during photosynthesis, but they do not use all of it. The plants release oxygen into the air through their leaves. Photosynthesis helps animals because animals need to breathe oxygen to survive.

Getting sun in a forest

Some forest plants get more sunlight than do other plants. Tall trees get a lot of sunlight. Their leaves block much of the sunlight from reaching the forest floor, however. As a result, the forest is dark under the big trees. Plants such as ferns, which grow on the forest floor, do not need much sunlight for photosynthesis. Small trees, shrubs, and **saplings**, or young trees, however, do need a lot of sunlight. To get enough sunlight, these plants grow quickly in spring, when the tall trees do not yet have leaves.

Forest plants

Forests are home to different kinds of plants. The largest plants are the tall trees that make up the forest. A variety of shrubs, ferns, mosses, wildflowers, and saplings also grow among the tall trees. Many plants grow in temperate forests because the soil is **fertile**, or full of nutrients.

The white trillium plant grows on the forest floor. It grows in early spring, before the leaves grow on the tall trees. As the leaves grow, less sunshine gets through to the forest floor.

Ferns survive on the forest floor because they need little sunlight for photosynthesis.

Changing with the seasons

To stay alive through the four seasons, the plants in temperate forests **adapt**, or change. In spring and summer, there is plenty of sunshine and water for plants to make food. In autumn, however, the days grow shorter and colder. There is not enough sunlight for broadleaved trees to make food. The leaves turn red, yellow, or orange because they no longer have chlorophyll to make them green. The leaves then fall off to save the trees energy. The trees become **dormant**—they are not active in winter. Without leaves or chlorophyll, the dormant trees cannot make food. They live off the food they have stored. The plants on the forest floor also become dormant in winter.

Forest herbivores

Many plants and animals live in temperate forests. Some forest animals, such as porcupines, are herbivores. Herbivores eat many plants every day to get the food energy they need.

Not all herbivores eat the same plants. Herbivores that eat leaves, twigs, and bark are called **browsers**. Those that eat grass and small plants near the ground are called **grazers**.

The beaver is a browser. It eats the leaves, twigs, and bark of trees that grow near water.

What do they eat?

Some herbivores eat only certain parts of plants. When forest flowers are in bloom, butterflies, bees, and many birds drink **nectar**. Nectar is a sweet liquid found in flowers. **Rodents** and some birds eat the seeds of plants. Many insects feed on fallen leaves. Other herbivores eat whichever plant parts they find, including fruits, roots, or nuts.

The white-tailed deer is both a browser and a grazer. During autumn and winter, it eats woody twigs. During spring and summer, it eats grasses, nuts, and fruits.

The gray squirrel eats fruits and nuts. In autumn, it collects these foods and stores them. The squirrel then finds these foods and eats them during winter.

15

Full of animals

Porcupines live near the forest floor in safe shelters, such as caves, but they climb trees to feed on nuts, berries, leaves, and bark.

*Skunks are **nocturnal**. Nocturnal animals sleep during the day and come out at night to hunt for food. Skunks spend their days sleeping in burrows.*

Forests are alive with animal life! Some animals use the tall trees as their homes, whereas others live on the forest floor. Birds, squirrels, and raccoons build nests among branches and in tree holes. Some animals do not live in trees, but they run up trees to hide from other animals.

The forest floor

Frogs and snakes live on the forest floor among tree roots and fallen leaves and branches. Groundhogs and rabbits protect themselves by living in underground tunnels called **burrows**.

16

Animals in four seasons

Animals that live in temperate forests must be able to adapt to the changing seasons. For example, porcupines eat leaves and grasses in summer and bark in winter. Many animals, such as squirrels, store extra food in autumn to make sure they have enough to last throughout winter. Some animals **migrate**, or travel long distances, to places with warm weather in winter. Other animals, such as frogs and snakes, stay in the forest year-round, but they **hibernate** so that their bodies can save energy. Frogs often hibernate in mud or in burrows.

Bears sleep through most of the winter, but they wake up on sunny, warm days and leave their dens to stretch.

17

Forest carnivores

Many animals that live in forests, including wolves, bobcats, and owls, are carnivores. Carnivores get food energy by eating other animals. Many carnivores are **predators**. Predators hunt and kill other animals for food. The animals that predators eat are called **prey**. Predators that eat herbivores are secondary consumers. Predators that eat other carnivores are called **tertiary consumers**.

Eating both kinds of animals

Some carnivores eat both herbivores and other carnivores. For example, when a fox eats a rabbit, which is a herbivore, the fox is a secondary consumer. When the fox eats a weasel, which is a carnivore, the fox is a tertiary consumer.

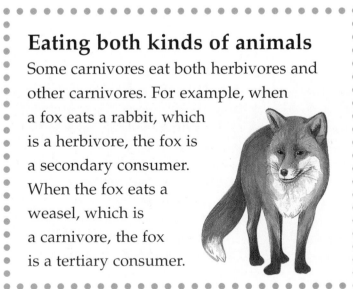

Weasels are carnivores. They eat small animals, including rabbits, mice, birds, and frogs.

Population control

Predators help control the **populations** of the animals they eat. For example, when wolves eat deer, they keep the deer population from becoming too big. If too many deer lived in a forest, all the plants would soon be eaten. The deer would also damage many trees by eating their bark.

Healthy food chains

Carnivores also help keep animal populations healthy. Carnivores usually hunt weak or sick animals because these animals are the easiest to catch. By hunting weak animals, carnivores remove them from a food chain. Without the weak animals, healthy animals have more food.

The eastern timber wolf hunts and eats deer, beavers, rabbits, and many kinds of rodents.

Hunting and scavenging

*Cougars **stalk**, or sneak close to, their prey and then quickly attack it by jumping out from behind bushes or jumping down from trees.*

Most forest predators have special body parts that help them hunt. Bald eagles, shown below, have excellent eyesight. They can spot prey from high in the sky. They then swoop down and grab the prey with their sharp **talons**.

On the forest floor, weasels **track**, or follow, rodents by listening for scurrying sounds and by using their good senses of smell. Weasels follow rodents to their burrows. Weasels have slim bodies that allow them to crawl right into the burrows!

Forest scavengers

Some carnivores are **scavengers**. Scavengers are animals that feed mainly on **carrion**, or dead animals. Skunks, opossums, and ants are all forest scavengers that eat dead insects, birds, and mammals.

Keeping forests clean

Scavengers help keep forests clean by eating dead animals that are on the forest floor. Scavengers also use the leftover food energy in the bodies of dead animals. Otherwise, this energy would go to waste.

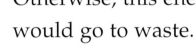

Red foxes are predators. They are also scavengers in winter, when their favorite foods are not available.

Forest omnivores

Many forest animals are **omnivores**—they get their energy by eating both animals and plants. Brown bears are omnivores. They eat berries, insects, fish, grass, and any other food they can find. Raccoons, skunks, and many birds are also omnivores.

They will eat anything!

Omnivores are **opportunistic feeders**. Opportunistic feeders are animals that eat any foods that are available. Omnivores do not have much trouble finding food because they eat almost anything!

Brown bears are excellent fishers! They often wade into rivers and catch fish. Brown bears also eat fruits, squirrels, and mice.

Foods in season

During autumn and winter in a temperate forest, there are fewer plants and animals to eat than there are in spring and summer. Many forest animals have become omnivores because omnivores are able to find food in every season. For example, cardinals, shown right, eat insects during summer and seeds during winter.

Raccoons come out at night to hunt for food. They eat frogs and fish, but they also eat nuts and fruits. They even eat foods that people have thrown away.

Forest clean-up crews

Decomposers also help keep forest floors clean. Decomposers are living things that eat dead plants and animals to get the energy that was stored in them. They also eat the animal parts that scavengers leave behind! Snails, earthworms, **bacteria**, and mushrooms are all decomposers.

Dead material

The diagram on the right shows how decomposers make up a **detritus food chain**. Detritus is material that is **decomposing,** or breaking down.

A detritus food chain

When a plant or an animal, such as this mouse, dies, it becomes dead material in the soil.

Decomposers, such as this earthworm, live in soil. Decomposers eat the dead material and get some of the energy stored in it. The decomposers then pass some of this energy into the soil through their droppings.

A decomposer's droppings add nutrients to the soil. The nutrients help new plants grow.

Note: The arrows point toward the living things that receive energy.

Healthy soil

Even after it is dead, a plant or an animal's body contains some energy. Decomposers use some of the energy, but not all of it. They put some of the leftover energy back into the soil through their droppings. The leftover energy contains nutrients that plants need to grow.

*A **fungus** is a plantlike living thing that feeds on dead plants and animals. Some common kinds of fungus are mushrooms and molds.*

Decomposers feed on dead leaves. As they feed, their bodies break down the leaves and put nutrients back into the soil. The nutrients help many types of plants grow in temperate forests.

25

A forest food web

Temperate forests contain many food chains. One food chain includes a plant, a herbivore, and a carnivore. Most living things belong to more than one food chain, however. When an animal from one food chain eats a plant or an animal from another food chain, two food chains connect. When two or more food chains connect, a **food web** is formed. Most food webs include many plants and animals.

A summer food web

This diagram shows a temperate forest food web during summer. The arrows point toward the living things that receive food energy.

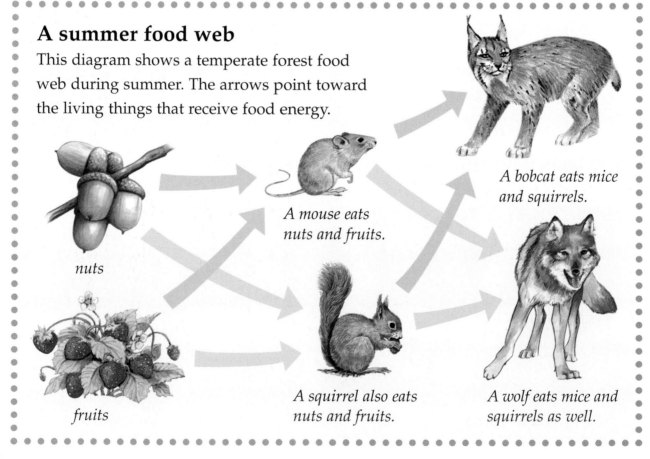

nuts

fruits

A mouse eats nuts and fruits.

A squirrel also eats nuts and fruits.

A bobcat eats mice and squirrels.

A wolf eats mice and squirrels as well.

Part-time plants

Temperate forest food webs change with the seasons. Some forest plants, including many kinds of wildflowers, grow for only part of the year. They are part of a food web only when they are growing. For example, the white-tailed deer, shown right, feeds on plants in spring and summer, while they are growing. In winter, the plants are covered with snow and are not part of the deer's diet. The deer eats tree bark instead.

Changing food webs

Animals that hibernate or migrate to new areas during winter do not eat in a forest. As a result, they are not part of winter food webs.

Ladybird beetles are not part of food webs in winter. Some ladybird beetles hibernate under rocks or tree roots. Others migrate to areas with warmer weather.

27

Enjoying forests

Respecting forests

You can enjoy forests without harming them! While hiking or biking, stay on marked trails to avoid destroying the plants or disturbing the animals. If you camp, use only areas of the forest that are set aside for camping. Campsites have fire pits. Fires can be lit safely in these marked-off areas. When the weather is dry or windy, campfires are usually not permitted. Obeying rules about campfires will keep both you and forests safe.

If campfires are permitted, make sure an adult lights the fire and then puts it out completely!

Recycle please!

Paper is made from trees. We can help save trees by **recycling** paper. Recycled paper products are made from waste paper instead of from trees. By using recycled paper products, you help reduce the number of trees that are cut down to make paper. Recycling paper instead of throwing it out also helps reduce the amount of garbage that is thrown into dumps.

Glossary

Note: Boldfaced words that are defined in the text may not appear in the glossary.

bacteria Tiny single-celled living things

energy The power living things get from food that helps them move, grow, and stay healthy

equator An imaginary line around the center of the Earth

hibernate To be in a sleeplike state during which the heart rate and breathing rate slow down

oxygen A colorless, odorless gas in the air that animals need to breathe

pigment A natural color found in plants and animals

population The total number of one type of plant or animal in a certain area

recycle To turn waste products into new products that can be used again

rodent An animal that has a small body and front teeth that never stop growing

talon A claw of a bird that is a carnivore

veins Tiny tubes that form the framework of a leaf and carry nutrients to the leaf

Index

1 2 3 4 5 6 7 8 9 0   Printed in the U.S.A.   4 3 2 1 0 9 8 7 6 5